GW01270056

WITHDRAWN

WITHDRAWN

Focus on

Jane Eyre

by Charlotte Brontë

Philip McCarthy

GREENWICH EXCHANGE
LONDON

Greenwich Exchange, London

Focus on
Jane Eyre
©Philip McCarthy 2012

First published in Great Britain in 2012
All rights reserved

This book is sold subject to the conditions that it shall not,
by way of trade or otherwise, be lent, resold, hired out or
otherwise circulated without the publisher's prior consent
in any form of binding or cover other than that in which it is
published and without a similar condition including this
condition being imposed on the subsequent purchaser.

Printed and bound by **imprint**digital.net
Typesetting and layout by Jude Keen Limited, London
Tel: 020 8355 4541
Cover design by December Publications, Belfast
Tel: 028 90286559

Greenwich Exchange Website: www.greenex.co.uk

Cataloguing in Publication Data is available
from the British Library.

ISBN: 978-1-906075-60-6

Contents

1

Introduction to *Jane Eyre*

A biographical sketch

It is a nice irony that Charlotte Brontë, whose life was spent in rural isolation and semi-obscurity should now be numbered with Shakespeare and Dickens among the international stars of English literature. Even those whose knowledge of novels is slight have heard of Emily Brontë's *Wuthering Heights* and Charlotte's *Jane Eyre*. The itinerary of literary tourists would be incomplete without a trip to the small Yorkshire village of Haworth, to pay homage at the vicarage and the rook-infested churchyard.

It was in 1820 that the Revd Patrick Brontë and his wife Maria, their five daughters and a son arrived in Haworth. Mr Brontë took up the position of vicar in the village church; the neighbouring vicarage (today the Brontë Museum) remained the family home throughout Charlotte's life. Although she and her sisters Emily and Anne left Haworth to attend school, to visit Belgium, to work as governesses, their excursions were short-lived and often unhappy. By contrast, in the enclosed world of the vicarage, near to the wild moors and with the companionship of siblings, they felt safe. In these surroundings they had the freedom to read widely and to exercise their imaginations, writing stories and creating imaginary kingdoms swept by wars, peopled with romantic heroes and heroines, riddled with intrigue.

Charlotte and her sisters served an apprenticeship to storytelling that was later to bear fruit in the successful publication of their novels. *Jane Eyre*, Charlotte's second novel, was published in three volumes in 1847, the same year as Thackeray's *Vanity Fair* and Emily Brontë's *Wuthering Heights*. It was an immediate success, drawing alike on the appeal of folk tales, romantic adventure and elements taken directly from her own experience: the stark realism of a brutal school and the unhappy working life of the governess.

It is significant that neither *Jane Eyre* nor *Wuthering Heights* appeared under the Brontës' own names. Charlotte published under the name Currer Bell and fiercely guarded the secret of her identity. This was no eccentricity but a practical measure to ensure that her work would be taken seriously. The French novelist George Sand (Aurore Dupin) had made the same decision before her, and George Eliot (Marian Evans) did the same a few years later. This sleight of hand is symptomatic of the restricted lives of women in the early 19th century. Male-dominated society held strong views on the matter. Women with time on their hands could write stories for the amusement of other women, but serious literature was a male preserve. The position of women in society is of special significance to us because in many ways it is the key concern of *Jane Eyre*. It is also the background to every other feature of the story.

The position of women

Often in discussions of Jane Austen's novels, readers wonder why her characters are so obsessed with marriage. It is a natural question, especially for young people who have grown up in a society in which marriage is merely one among many available choices, and the right of women to pursue a career, to own property and to determine their own way of life is taken for granted. The reason of course is that in the England of the early 19th century women had no such rights and very few options.

A large percentage of working-class women worked outside the home as a matter of necessity, both before and after marriage. In the year 1841 55 per cent of working women were employed as servants. A further large percentage worked in the cotton mills, and a smaller number in male-dominated industries such as mining.

Much of their labour was drudgery of the wretched sort, with poor pay and excessive hours, but at least access to work gave working-class women a small measure of freedom, something denied to their middle-class sisters. Middle-class women, like Charlotte Brontë and Jane Austen before her, had little future outside marriage. They could be highly intelligent, well educated and curious about life; but they could not go to universities, enter the professions or own property. It is small wonder, then, that a good marriage was vital. This is not to belittle the positive and natural desire of men and women to find love and build a life together; but that is a very different impulse from women's need to marry at all costs, which is a key element of the Jane Austen world.

With few exceptions, unmarried middle-class women in the early 19th century were to be found either keeping house for their relatives or working as governesses. Both options were familiar to Charlotte Brontë and both equally unattractive. Her own aunt provided a first-hand example of the housekeeper. She came to take care of the Brontë children after their mother's death and dedicated the remainder of her life to their welfare. It was a mutually supportive arrangement: she was provided with a home and security, while they were tended and fed. All three Brontë sisters had worked as governesses, and Charlotte was able to write with real empathy about that life.

The governess inhabited an ambiguous territory between the family upstairs and the downstairs realm of the servants. She was often better educated than her employers, but she was not treated as an equal. The governess was influential in bringing up the children, but she was not their mother. She was, in essence, a servant, at the beck and call of her masters. She must be careful not to give herself airs or to compete with the ladies of the family. As an unmarried woman, she could be seen as a sexual competitor to her mistress and a temptation to her master.

Experience varied of course from household to household; but in extreme cases, a governess had to put up with the tantrums of the children, the whims and patronising treatment of her master and mistress, and the pity or contempt of their friends. For every governess whose world was comfortable, kind and fulfilled there were many who endured a harsh, stifling existence.

The reality of the governess in the 19th century made her a familiar figure in contemporary debate about women in society, and an equally familiar figure in fiction. Her ambivalent status gave her a rich fictional potential, especially perhaps in the realm of romance and wish-fulfilment. The position of governess is the ideal vehicle for moving a genteel but poor heroine into a place where she can meet and marry a wealthy widower. Apart from *Jane Eyre*, the most famous example is Becky Sharp in *Vanity Fair*. Thackeray's intention is not romance but satire. Becky, the keen-witted ambitious social climber, has no wealth or connections, but she uses her position as governess to move in high society, playing on people's weaknesses to get what she wants. Even in Jane Austen's work, in which governesses are not prominent, there are minor characters in this position, finding a romance that promotes them to lady of the manor.[1] Charlotte Brontë, however, was probably the first novelist to present in fiction what it felt like to be a governess, with all the frustrations and limitations of the position, and to reveal the dissatisfaction of many women at the lack of opportunity in their lives.

What the reviewers saw

When Jane Eyre came out in 1847 the reviews were mostly good. William Thackeray and George Lewes, two of the most influential literary men of the day, were enthusiastic. The majority of reviewers found the novel emotionally powerful, original in its treatment of its subject and full of natural energy. Many speculated on whether the author was a woman or a man, and also on the presentation of the story as autobiographical. Melodramatic incidents (the final fire) and weak portrayal of character (St John Rivers) were noted, but generally seen as minor blemishes. Some critics praised the novel for showing that integrity can overcome social disadvantages.

Others disliked *Jane Eyre*, commenting on the coarseness of language and the characters' behaviour. Critics who were disturbed by the relationship of Jane and Rochester were matched by others who saw the treatment of religious hypocrisy and social inequality as anti-Christian and subversive:

> We do not hesitate to say that the tone of mind and thought which has overthrown authority and violated every code human and divine abroad, and fostered Chartism and rebellion at home, is the same which has also written *Jane Eyre*.[2]

Charlotte Brontë thought this reviewer's opinion unjust, and she wrote to say so. The judgement is extreme, but there was widespread fear of revolution at the time; the revival of Chartist demands for radical change and the spread of socialist ideas on the Continent made many people uneasy. The reviewer does at least identify the characteristic that every discerning reader of *Jane Eyre* is aware of: the anger and passion that inspire the story.

Charlotte Brontë is indeed a rebellious and angry writer. More generally, she is attempting, like the Romantic poets, to find ways of expressing in language the mysterious area of human emotions beneath the civilised and rational surface, emotions that cannot be properly conveyed in the dialogue and reflections of Jane Austen's heroines, feelings that are often wild and disturbing. It is the emotional landscape of Coleridge's 'Ancient Mariner' or of Emily Brontë's *Wuthering Heights*, where a civilised traveller is woken by an apparition at his window, pulls a cold hand through the glass and rubs the wrist on the jagged edge till it bleeds. One could not imagine this kind of melodramatic episode in Jane Austen; but something similar is at work in *Jane Eyre*, for example in the figure of the madwoman locked in the attic.

* * *

In the sections that follow I shall discuss Charlotte Brontë's presentation of Jane, searching like a pilgrim for acceptance and recognition. I shall go on to consider the tension between nature and control, which is central to the story. Some of the ways in which women are presented will form a separate discussion. I shall focus briefly on the exploration of the heroine's feelings and conclude with a consideration of the competing demands of realism and romance. In the course of these discussions we shall also touch on the influence of fairy tale, Brontë's use of imagery and symbol, and the force of her social criticism.

All the quotations, with page references, are taken from the World's Classics edition of *Jane Eyre* edited by Margaret Smith. This is based on the Clarendon edition of 1969, and follows the text of the first (1847) edition. It has the advantages of being accurate, widely available and not expensive.

NOTES

1   In Jane Austen's *Emma*, published in 1816, the heroine's governess, Miss Taylor, and the enigmatic Jane Fairfax are examples.

2   Elizabeth Rigby, writing in the *Quarterly Review* (1848). See Sara Lodge, *Charlotte Brontë – Jane Eyre: A Reader's Guide to Essential Criticism* (2009), chapter 1 for a full account of Victorian criticism of *Jane Eyre*.

2

The Search for Acceptance

It is clear from the opening paragraphs of *Jane Eyre* that Charlotte Brontë intends to present Jane as a child who does not feel accepted by her aunt and guardian, Mrs Reed. Her aunt, like a fairy-tale stepmother, keeps the interloper at a distance while she dotes uncritically on her own three children, John, Eliza and Georgiana. Jane is introduced as a sad girl, humbled by a belief in her physical inferiority and conscious that any chance of joining the family circle depends on her transformation into the idealised child that Mrs Reed demands. She must "acquire a more sociable and child-like disposition, a more attractive and sprightly manner, – something lighter, franker, more natural" (p.7). In other words, she must stop being Jane Eyre and become someone completely different.

The quest for acceptance begins here, with the ten-year-old Jane looking in on the warm, happy existence of her cousins but not feeling part of it. The novel follows the life of the heroine, told in the first person, as she moves through five distinct phases, growing to womanhood and searching for fulfilment. The first phase presents her years at Gateshead Hall, the home of the Reed family; the second describes Jane's time at the grim charity school at Lowood. This period is followed by the transforming period at Thornfield, as governess to Adèle, interrupted only by a return visit to Gateshead to see the dying Mrs Reed. The fourth phase is Jane's flight from Thornfield with an alternative future offered by the Rivers family. The fifth and final section is her return to Thornfield, where her destiny is settled.

Childhood at Gateshead Hall
The Brontës were strongly influenced by folk and fairy tales. Jane Eyre is a Cinderella figure, a child with an unfeeling stepmother and cruel siblings. The perennial appeal of the story comes not only from the familiarity of the fairy tale, but also from the universal and timeless emotion of sibling rivalry. The powerful passions that it can generate are

presented in their rawest form as the children quarrel, taunt and fight. The adult who should be there to comfort, Mrs Reed, automatically supports her own children and leaves Jane isolated and sad.

Sadness is the first emotion attributed to Jane. She is the intruder, watching, like Cinderella, as the significant life is lived by other people, whose attitude is hostile. Not even the servants, who might have taken a more balanced view, can spare much pity for her:

> "If she were a nice pretty child one might compassionate her forlornness; but one really cannot care for such a little toad as that." "Not a great deal, to be sure," agreed Bessie: "at any rate a beauty like miss Georgiana would be more moving in the same condition." (p.26)

It is little wonder that her favoured strategy is to cut herself off from a society she is forbidden to join. She is happiest behind a drawn curtain in the window seat, escaping as best she can into an imagined world conjured up by books:

> Folds of scarlet drapery shut in my view to the right hand; to the left were the clear panes of glass protecting, but not separating me from the drear November day. At intervals, while turning over the leaves of my book, I studied the aspect of that winter afternoon. Afar it offered a pale blank of mist and cloud; near a scene of wet lawn and storm-beat shrub, with ceaseless rain sweeping away wildly before a long and lamentable blast. (p.8)

On one side the scarlet curtain seems to suggest the warmth and life of the family she cannot join, while on the other, the natural world beyond the window is pale, chaotic and miserable.

It is suggestive of the state of her feelings; as indeed is the vast landscape of ice and rock that she imagines as she reads the description in Bewick's *History of British Birds*. She pictures dreary expanses of ice and frost, shadowy "death-white realms", and the associated feelings, sombre and impressive, transfer themselves to the illustrations that follow: pictures of isolated rocks, wave-beaten coasts, wrecked vessels, graveyards and horned devils. Brontë is using these landscapes, as she uses the storm beyond the window, to help suggest the isolated and colourless quality of Jane's existence; but she is also showing, through Jane's interest in the book, a mind absorbed and fascinated by images whose mysterious qualities recall for her the fairy tales and ballads told at bedtime by her nurse Bessie. There is a hidden life, a hidden Jane who waits to emerge, a Jane fascinated by mystery, colour, love and adventure. It is this imagination, shaping and colouring her drawings, that catches the eye of Rochester later in the novel (see pp.125-6).

Injustice

If sadness and isolation are the first keynotes, then persecution and injustice follow close behind. The chief agents are the Reed children, especially John, a fourteen-year-old bully, who delights in torturing Jane like an insect. It is John who forces her from the window seat to be the butt of his insults and violence. Any attempt on Jane's part to strike back is turned against her. The nurses and the children, as well as Mrs Reed herself, all treat her as the instigator, the sneaky troublemaker. It is Jane who is punished for the behaviour of the others. Her smouldering sense of injustice explodes into angry protest; but this only increases the severity of punishment.

These emotions are focused by the 'red-room' episode. After the violent quarrel with John she is carried there by the servants, kicking and struggling. Brontë emphasises her isolation by providing no sympathetic allies. Both Bessie and Miss Abbott criticise her behaviour and remind her that she is not the equal of the Reeds but in danger of being sent away unless she becomes more biddable. It is interesting that she objects violently to the idea that John Reed is her young master: "Master! How is he my master? Am I a servant?" (p.12). Jane may be an outsider, but she is not prepared to accept injustice without protest. She is not a slave; she rebels. Later in the story she is prepared to use the word 'master' with very different emotions, but not here: "my blood was still warm; my mood of the revolted slave was still bracing me with its bitter vigour" (p.14).

Jane is locked into the 'red-room'. It is a vast bedchamber with damask draperies, red carpet and massive mahogany woodwork. By contrast the bed, table and chairs present an expanse of intense white. The colour scheme reflects the colours in the window seat; and in fact throughout the novel many of the key emotional scenes occur in a frame of red and white. It is as if Jane is caught between two stark areas of emotion: the warmth, passion, anger, blood and violence of the crimsons and the pallid, colourless lifelessness of white.

The red chamber is an oppressive place with sinister associations. It is the place where Mr Reed died and was laid in his coffin. It is the place sacred to the memory of a dead husband, where mementoes and old documents are kept in secret drawers. One can read in these settings the influence of the Gothic novel[1] with its grim castles and dark, ghostly chambers. It is not long in fact before Jane, as darkness falls and the wind howls outside, begins to think of the dead Mr Reed, wondering whether his ghost may be disturbed by her treatment and her grief:

> I dwelt on it with gathering dread. *(p.16)*

> I wiped my tears and hushed my sobs; fearful lest any sign of violent grief might waken a preternatural voice to comfort me ... This idea, consolatory in theory, I felt would be terrible if realised. *(p.17)*

Charlotte Brontë skilfully evokes the fertile imagination of this young child locked into the cold and dismal mausoleum. As the idea of visiting spirits fixes itself in her mind and the darkness settles in the room, her terror increases. A streak of light playing across the ceiling drives her to near-panic. Believing that it heralds a vision from another world she rushes to the locked door and yells for help; but in spite of some sympathy from Bessie, the harsh voice of Mrs Reed condemns her to stay in the chamber, where she falls into a fit.

The red-room episode also allows Brontë to show Jane brooding on her own character and treatment. The sense of injustice is deep:

> Why was I always suffering, always brow-beaten, always accused, for ever condemned? ... I dared to commit no fault: I strove to fulfil every duty; and I was termed naughty and tiresome, sullen and sneaking, from morning to noon, and from noon to night ...
> "Unjust! – unjust!" said my reason. *(p.17)*

But from brooding on injustice Jane turns to the more hurtful sense of rejection. The young child cannot fully understand; but the adult Jane, who is telling the story, breaks in with her thoughts, recognising the child's insecurities but willing also to understand the difficulty of the widowed Mrs Reed, forced to take on a child she did not want and could not love.

A loving adult
There is a skilful continuity as Brontë moves us, with the semi-conscious Jane, out of the red-room. The imagined support of the ghostly Mr Reed is replaced by the real help of Mr Lloyd, the physician. It is clear that Jane needs the security of a strong, loving adult, in this case a father figure:

… he departed; to my grief: I felt so sheltered and befriended while he sat in the chair near my pillow; and as he closed the door after him, all the room darkened and my heart again sank: inexpressible sadness weighed it down. (p.19)

A further aspect of the red-room episode is worth emphasising. As Jane glances at her reflection in the looking-glass, gazing into its depths, she is fascinated by the otherworldly appearance of the figure looking back: "I thought it like one of those tiny phantoms, half fairy half imp, Bessie's evening stories represented as coming up out of lone ferny dells" (p.14). This imagery is taken up later in the novel by Rochester, who constantly sees her in the same light.

Any reader familiar with *Wuthering Heights* will recall the way in which Heathcliff is also introduced and described as a fairy child or changeling, who appears in the household and becomes the focus of sibling envy and destruction. Jane too has been brought into a household like a cuckoo child and the rest of the family forced to accept her.

Miserable and unloved, Jane's only consolation is in the world of books; but after the searing episode of the red-room she learns that powerful feelings can destroy even that enjoyable escape:

> when this cherished volume was now placed in my hand – when I turned over its leaves, and sought in its marvellous pictures the charm I had, till now, never failed to find – all was eerie and dreary; the giants were gaunt goblins, the pigmies malevolent and fearful imps … I closed the book, which I dared no longer peruse. (p.21)

At such times only the mournful singing of Bessie chimes in a morbid way with her gloom as she listens to 'The Poor Orphan Child'.

Direct and honest

If sadness is the keynote of the young Jane's character, it is not her most memorable quality. The most striking, and in a way amusing characteristic is her passionate directness and honesty. If she disagrees she will say so because she is fired by anger and resentment. When the kindly apothecary returns, Bessie suggests that she is crying because she was not allowed to ride in the carriage. Jane's self-esteem will not endure this: "I never cried for such a thing in my life: I hate going out in the carriage. I cry because I am miserable" (pp.22-3). Later, when Mrs Reed tells young John not to associate with her, Jane shouts over the banister: "They are not fit to associate with me" (p.27), and then, experiencing the wrath of her stepmother:

"What would Uncle Reed say to you if he were alive?"

"My Uncle Reed is in heaven and can see all you do and think; and so can papa and mama: they know how you shut me up all day long, and how you wish me dead." (ibid.)

Plain Jane is judged only by her appearance, but the mistreatment she endures strengthens her sense of injustice and her rebellious spirit. When the hypocritical Brocklehurst comes to discuss her removal to school, Mrs Reed poisons his mind, in the presence of the watching Jane, with the idea that she is a liar. The victim cannot hold back:

I am not deceitful: if I were I should say I loved you; but I declare, I do not love you: I dislike you the worst of anybody in the world except John Reed; and this book about the liar, you may give to your girl, Georgiana, for it is she who tells lies, and not I. (p.36)

Brontë brings the first phase of Jane's life to a resounding conclusion by allowing this ugly, watchful outsider, this bullied orphan, to express her true feelings with freedom and passion to her chief persecutor:

I am glad you are no relation of mine: I will never call you aunt again as long as I live. I will never come to see you when I am grown up; and if anyone asks me how I liked you, and how you treated me, I will say the very thought of you makes me sick, and that you treated me with miserable cruelty. (p.36)

Schooldays

Jane is shown leaving Gateshead in a positive cast of mind, as if the doors have closed on a prison and she is happy to escape. But she is alone. There is no parent or caring guardian to journey with her. She was not accepted at Gateshead and the search for acceptance continues. Underlying it is the yearning for love, the unconditional love of a father, mother or friend whom she can love in return. At Gateshead the only object of her affection is a battered doll: "Human beings must love something, and in the dearth of worthier objects of affection I contrived to find a pleasure in loving and cherishing a faded graven image, shabby as a miniature scarecrow" (p.38).

The first impression of the school is provided by the tall, grave lady, Miss Temple, who comments in surprise that this child should have been allowed to travel alone. She speaks kindly and turns out to be genuinely concerned for fairness and justice. The burnt porridge, for example, is replaced at her order, although Brocklehurst reprimands her for the action.

Both Jane and Helen Burns regard Miss Temple with a mixture of awe and admiration. She moves and works with dignity and quiet authority, and bends the strict rules imposed upon her when she can. She is the opposite of Mrs Reed in her treatment of the underdogs: "Miss Temple is full of goodness; it pains her to be severe to any one, even the worst in the school," says Helen (p.56), in an attitude of hero worship that Jane comes to share.

If Miss Temple represents the parent that Jane never had, then Helen Burns becomes the surrogate sister and Jane develops a strong friendship with her. Her character, based on Charlotte Brontë's own sister, is presented as an example of a particular kind of Christianity: passive endurance in the face of persecution.

Although these strengthening relationships lie at the heart of the Lowood experience, they are the bright foils that serve to emphasise the prevailing darkness, cruelty and hypocrisy. Jane has left Gateshead only to enter an institution that imprisons her once more. It is run according to an evangelical style of Christianity which views children as sinners whose impulses, even the most playful, creative and tender, must be constrained and chastised.

The dark side of education

The relationship between Jane and Helen may provide the central character interest, but for many readers the most fascinating aspect of this section is the realistic presentation that it gives of an early 19th-century school, derived from Brontë's own experience as a teacher.

When Brocklehurst appears at the school on one of his regular visits, Brontë takes the opportunity to criticise, through his speech and behaviour, the hypocrisy of his supposed Christianity. He rebukes Miss Temple for serving the children two meals of bread and cheese; and when told that this resulted from a burned breakfast, he produces an attempt at religious argument to support his view: "You are aware that my plan in bringing up these girls is, not to accustom them to habits of luxury and indulgence but to render them hardy, patient, self-denying" (p.62). The extremism of his views would make him a comic figure had he not, like so many Dickensian villains, the well-being of powerless people in his hands. He complains not only about replacing the burnt meal but also about seeing holed stockings on the line and about too many clean dresses being given out. Brontë leaves the reader to decide whether these complaints stem from religious fervour or simple meanness. In later years, when Jane is talking to Mrs Fairfax, it is clear which view she holds.[2] Brocklehurst is the enemy not only of genuine care and compassion, but also of what is natural and individual. When he notices girls with curly hair he is appalled. When Miss Temple tells him that Julia's hair curls naturally he finds his theme: "Naturally! Yes but we are not here to conform to nature; I wish these girls to be the children of grace" (p.64). He insists that the girl's hair is cut off immediately.

Brontë is good at bringing out the comedy of this puritanical zeal in speeches using religious language to justify mean-minded cruelty:

Madam … I have a master to serve whose kingdom is not of this world; my mission is to mortify in these girls the lusts of the flesh; to teach them to clothe themselves with shamefacedness and sobriety, not with braided hair and costly apparel; and each of the young persons before us has a string of hair twisted in plaits which vanity itself might have woven. (p.64)

Although Helen Burns does not feel the direct lash of Brocklehurst's tongue she suffers at the hands of teachers. Miss Scatcherd is constantly critical of Helen, in spite of the girl's intelligence and outstanding performance in class. Jane watches in amazement as the teacher fails to praise her excellent grasp of lessons and picks instead on externals: "You dirty, disagreeable girl! You have never cleaned your nails this morning" (p.53). The misdemeanour results in a caning. Jane witnesses this injustice and Brontë presents her after the cruel episode wandering restlessly among the noisy children, alone but not lonely, and listening with relish to the voice of nature beyond the window. It is as if the unjust treatment of Helen has raised in Jane a fellow-feeling and rebellious emotions that are echoed in her surroundings: "I derived from both a strange excitement, and reckless and feverish, I wished the wind to howl more wildly, the gloom to deepen to darkness, and the confusion to rise to clamour" (p.55). But if Jane expects Helen to share her rebellious passion she is disappointed, and receives instead a lesson in patience and quiet endurance.

Helen Burns

Since her arrival at Lowood, Jane has watched Helen but communicated little; now she breaks the habit and speaks to the other girl, who is concentrating on a book. As readers, we feel that Jane is looking for a fellow rebel after the cruel treatment she has seen Helen receive. Like herself, Helen is an outsider interested in books. Helen's book, however, is not to Jane's more romantic taste; it is *Rasselas* by Samuel Johnson, a philosophical text concerned with the meaning of life and the nature of the good life. The heroine is in fact more concerned with the afterlife than with life on earth, and this preoccupation fits the otherworldly character of Helen Burns. Helen is constantly criticised by the teachers, for not remembering, for untidiness, for lateness; but she accepts it all without protest, taking Christ as her model. She instructs Jane in morality, opposing the idea that one should strike back and resist evil. She mildly reprimands Jane for her grudge against Mrs Reed and advises her to forget. She accepts her own sufferings at the hands of Miss Scatcherd without protest: "No ill usage so brands its record on my feelings. Would you not be happier if you tried to forget her severity, together with the passionate emotion it excited?" (p.58). The presentation of Helen does at times seem a little artificial and preachy, but Charlotte Brontë herself, faced with this criticism insisted that the character, based on her own sister, was totally true to life. In any event Helen is a girl who is inspired by Christianity. The irony is that she is persecuted by the very people who profess to be the representatives of Christian morality.

Endurance and rebellion

When Jane rebelliously tells Helen that in her place she would have broken the cane under Miss Scatcherd's nose, she is shocked by the other girl's response: "Yet it would be your duty to bear it, if you could not avoid it: it is weak and silly to say you cannot bear what is your fate to be required to bear." Jane is amazed:

> I heard her with wonder: I could not comprehend this doctrine of endurance; and still less could I understand or sympathize with the forbearance she expressed for her chastiser. Still I felt that Helen Burns considered things by a light invisible to my eyes. I suspected that she might be right and I wrong. (p.56)

Brontë shows Jane receiving a moral and spiritual education from Helen; and yet, while Jane is clearly impressed, the reader may feel that she is not completely convinced.

For the highest of motives Helen seems to acquiesce too easily in a discipline that does not recognise her distinctive nature but seeks to confine and destroy it. Jane cannot accept that punishment is always for the victim's good and that injustice must be endured. When Miss Scatcherd ties a placard round Helen's forehead with the word 'slattern' written on it and forces the girl to wear it through the day, Jane boils with outrage and takes the first opportunity to tear the card from her friend's head. She is all the more upset because Helen bears this cruelty with resignation.

When the school suffers an outbreak of typhus, Brontë makes it clear that bad food and neglect have brought about the epidemic. Helen becomes seriously ill with that other killer disease so familiar to the Victorians, tuberculosis (or consumption as it was called). After a dramatic but sentimental scene, Helen dies, with Jane sharing the deathbed. The reader is left with the sense that the author has established Helen both as a moral exemplar for Jane and as a model of true Christianity, against which the superficial and hypocritical religiosity of Brocklehurst and his like can be measured. Religious and social criticism combine in these chapters to denounce the inhumanity of many of the charity schools of the age and the hypocrisy of the seemingly pious men who ran them.

Documentary detail

After the death of Helen Burns, Brontë moves forward several years, reporting that the terrible conditions at Lowood had been mitigated. The exposure of the children's sufferings has caused benefactors to come forward and provide a better building in a healthier place. Although Brocklehurst remains, he has lost his power; the school has improved and its educational standards have risen.

The presentation of Lowood and the fate of girls like Helen Burns are based very closely on the experience of Charlotte herself.[2] Lowood is Cowan Bridge, the school for clergymen's daughters attended by Charlotte and her sisters. Brocklehurst is based on the Revd William Wilson, its founder:

> Charlotte raged not only against her own physical and mental suffering at Cowan Bridge. Her charge against the institution was far more severe, for quite literally she blamed Mr Wilson's school for the deaths of [her two elder sisters] Elizabeth and Maria. (Peters, *Unquiet Soul*, p.11)

The power of the Lowood chapters depends on the convincing documentary detail, and this documentary aspect was recognised by Victorian readers, who were appalled at the condition it exposed:

> When Jane Eyre was published, Lowood was immediately identified as Cowan Bridge – much to Charlotte's consternation – and a great cry of indignation went up from Mr Wilson's friends and the many distinguished patrons of the school. (ibid., p.15)

Margot Peters goes on to suggest that her schooldays had determined in Charlotte a capacity for seething resentment beneath a surface of quiet, obedience and hard work.

After the marriage of Miss Temple, Jane finds that her motive for quiet and contentment has gone. Her restlessness returns. The significant adult in her life, the mother figure who kept her calm and focused, has moved away. The school, like Gateshead House, seems like a prison and increasingly Jane longs for freedom to "Seek real knowledge of life amidst its perils" (p.85). "I desired liberty; for liberty I gasped; for liberty I uttered a prayer ... 'Then,' I cried, half desperate, 'grant me at least a new servitude!'" (ibid.).

Governess at Thornfield
Jane's move to Thornfield is a leap into the dark. She has spent eight years at Lowood, including the last two as a teacher. She has become an educated young woman, but has no home or family. The only way she can support herself is to become a private governess. The fact that Thornfield is seventy miles nearer London recommends the offered position to her: "I longed to go where there was life and movement" (p.89).

A Gothic hall
The influence on Brontë of Gothic tales can be read in the rambling neglected hall set in a lonely place. The interior has some cosy and warm corners, but it is also heavy, gloomy and cold:

> The steps and banisters were of oak, the staircase window was high and latticed: both it and the long gallery into which the bedroom doors opened looked as if they belonged to a church rather than a house. A very chill and vault-like air pervaded the stairs and gallery, suggesting cheerless ideas of space and solitude. (p.97)

Jane's new search for acceptance begins against this dramatic background.

If Jane's childhood draws on the influence of Cinderella, then the Thornfield episode feels more like 'Beauty and the Beast' or 'Bluebeard'.[3] A young girl enters a lonely, mysterious castle which holds a fearful secret.

Initially however Jane's attention is taken by Mrs Fairfax, whom she imagines to be an unusually friendly employer, and of course by Adèle.

Apart from these relationships, the main impression is one of mystery. Jane admits to feeling afraid of the night. Ghosts are mentioned. The attic corridor is dark and strange, and Jane is shocked to hear laughter drifting from one of the locked rooms, laughter that is later attributed to the shadowy Grace Poole. Brontë has Jane comparing the corridor on the third floor to Bluebeard's Castle (p.107), raising in the reader the possibility that, as in that tale, some horrific secret may be hidden behind the locked doors.

This Gothic atmosphere is firmly established, and its mystery clings not only to the hall itself but also gathers around the character of its owner, Mr Rochester. On realising that Mrs Fairfax is only the housekeeper, Jane is full of questions regarding Rochester and fascinated by the brief but enigmatic sketch that she receives, of a man much travelled in the world, who returns occasionally and always unexpectedly to the house, a man peculiar and difficult to fathom – in other words a man of mystery. Routine establishes itself, and Jane increasingly feels lonely and discontented: "I valued what was good in Mrs Fairfax, and what was good in Adèle, but I believed in the existence of other more vivid kinds of goodness and what I believed in I wished to behold" (p.109). This is partly a roundabout way of suggesting that this young woman would value some male companionship; but more important is the reassertion that Jane, beneath the quiet exterior, has a vitality and restless passion that this monotonous existence cannot satisfy. She longs for life and sees only stagnation. It is significant that she finds an outlet for her pent-up emotion walking the corridor where from time to time she hears the strange laughter of Grace Poole.

Rochester

This mood of restless discontent is broken by the sudden arrival of Rochester. Jane is walking in the evening, enjoying the rural solitude like a character in a Wordsworth poem, when she hears the sound of a horse approaching at speed. Unknown to Jane, it is Rochester who is galloping into the novel. His horse slips on icy ground, he takes a fall, and this leads to a meeting with Jane. It is not a romantic occasion, although Jane at first associates the sound and the dog with ghostly tales. The gentleman curses roundly, and because he needs help and is not a handsome charmer, Jane is not intimidated. She finds the man striking but not beautiful, with his stern features, heavy brow and angry eyes. Regarding herself as plain, Jane feels comfortable with the grim-looking Rochester and is happy to offer help. It is significant that the meeting livens her mood, only to have it deadened once more by her return to Thornfield: "The incident had occurred and was gone for me, it was an incident of no moment, no romance, no interest in a sense; yet it marked with change one single hour of a monotonous life" (p.115). It is only some time later when called into the presence of the owner that Jane recognises Rochester as the strange horseman. In her characteristic position of watching unseen, she notes the grim features with some satisfaction and concludes that he is more remarkable for character than for beauty. (The idea that human beauty is not of itself worthy of praise is a repeated theme in the novel.)

The character of Rochester owes much to the Romantic Byronic hero of the early 19th century.[4] He is no typical gentleman with smooth manners, good looks and conventional ideas. Like Byron himself and the heroes of his poems, Rochester is a man with a mysterious past, weighed down with the burden of some dark guilt. He has travelled the world and lived life to the full, but he does not trouble to ingratiate himself with others. His speech is to the point, often abrupt and sometimes sarcastic. Rochester is a man of energy and action, but he is essentially enigmatic, and it is this complex, mysterious quality that holds the reader's and of course Jane Eyre's attention. One might compare him with the much darker and demonic character of Heathcliff, created by Charlotte's sister Emily. The Byronic model is the same, but while Heathcliff becomes a symbol or a force of nature, Rochester remains recognisably human.

The longing for life
The terrible longing for life, however undefined in detail, grows in intensity as Jane returns from her evening encounter to re-enter the hall: "I did not like re-entering Thornfield. To pass its threshold was to return to stagnation" (p.116).

With the arrival of Rochester, life returns to the Hall. It bustles with activity, it rings with sound. Visitors come and go. The new atmosphere dissolves Jane's restless discontent: "A rill from the outer world was flowing through it. It had a master: for my part I liked it better" (p.118). It is not just the stream of life that brings new contentment to Jane; it is the presence of a strong, controlling figure, the master, hopefully a kind one, who will reflect in his concern and acceptance those influential figures from the past: the doctor, Miss Temple, Uncle Reed and the father she never knew.

Although Rochester is abrupt and direct in his comments to Jane, he is honest and he is interested, and Jane is comfortable in his company and able to respond with equal honesty to his questions. The sharp honesty that Jane displayed in the Reed household was not emphasised in the school chapters, but here it returns, not because of Rochester's hostility but because of his interest.

Obstacles to romance

Jane's habit of watchfulness is focused on Rochester. She is very aware of his changing moods but she is not concerned, knowing that she is not the cause.

Rochester's interest in Jane is clear, as he invites her to sit close and talk to him. Blunt himself, he approves of her directness. He is not offended by her plain reply of 'no' when asked whether she considers him handsome. Jane, on the other hand will be ordered to talk, and her response draws from him an apology and an admission that he wants to talk to her as an equal.

Jane has found the mentor who will accept her and see her true value. Brontë raises for the reader the expectation of romance and fulfilment, in this grim place, with its frowning owner. One can read the influence of 'Beauty and the Beast' behind the story.

There are still major obstacles in the way of a complete realisation. The first problem raised in their conversation is the fact that Jane is only a servant, and however much Rochester wishes to talk to her as an equal, he is still the master and still able to give her orders.

In spite of this they become companions; Rochester confides in Jane, talking about his past, including his relationship with Céline, Adèle's mother, and at times suggesting to Jane that she is capable of refreshing his life, as if the stain of experience can be washed away by her innocence: "The more you and I converse, the better, for while I cannot blight you, you may refresh me" (p.143). Rochester unburdens himself of many secrets, his feeling of regret, his world-weariness, his conviction that he is weighed down by sin, his passion to taste pleasure once more.

In presenting Jane as his confidante, Brontë is both giving substance to his Byronic character and showing how she is gradually growing closer, becoming dependent emotionally on his presence and attention:

The ease of his manner freed me from painful restraint: the friendly frankness, as correct as cordial, with which he treated me, drew me to him. I felt at times, as if he were my relation, rather than my master: yet he was imperious sometimes still; but I did not mind that; I saw it was his way. So happy, so gratified did I become with this new interest added to life, that I ceased to pine after kindred: my thin crescent destiny seemed to enlarge; the blanks of my existence were filled up; my bodily health improved; I gathered flesh and strength.

And was Mr Rochester now ugly in my eyes? No, reader: gratitude, and many associations, all pleasurable and genial, made his face the object I liked best to see: his presence in a room was more cheering than the brightest fire. (p.146)

Jane is clearly falling in love with Rochester in their growing intimacy, her happiness and the disappearance of her old feeling of incompleteness. And in the timeless way of romantic love the object of her love loses his ugliness and becomes the bright sun of her world.

Although Rochester's feelings are not made explicit, after the fire episode, he is passionate in his talk with Jane, who has saved his life; and his disturbed and broken speech suggests more than mere gratitude. The fact that they are alone at the dead of night in his bedroom is intended to give a *frisson* of romantic expectation to the reader:

Strange energy was in his voice; strange fire in his look.
"I am glad I happened to be awake," I said; and then I was going.
"What! you will go?" (p.151)

Rochester's intensity is matched in this climactic episode by Jane's own emotion. Natural imagery is used to suggest the confusion of feelings as happiness and disquiet battle for supremacy: "Till morning dawned I was tossed on a buoyant but unquiet sea, where billows of trouble rolled under surges of joy" (ibid.). This blend of joyful anticipation and disturbance warns the reader that the road to fulfilment will not be an easy one.

Blanche Ingram
This impression is reinforced immediately by the visit to Thornfield of the Ingram family, and in particular by the character of Blanche, who seems marked out by her beauty and accomplishment to be the future wife of Rochester.

The visit of the local grandees is a significant event. It shows Jane directly acknowledging her love for Rochester, if only to herself. Faced with the elegance and easy confidence of Blanche Ingram, she can only compare herself unfavourably; and seeing what she takes to be Rochester's courtship, she admits to a feeling of loss: "I must, then, repeat continually that we are for ever sundered: – and yet, while I breathe and think, I must love him" (p.175). But although Jane is forced to acknowledge her own feelings, the reader can only speculate about Rochester's motives. Is he trying to distance himself from Jane and making a genuine attempt to court Blanche? Is he testing Jane in some way? The unconvincing episode in which, disguised as a gypsy, he interviews Jane suggests that he is testing her; but we learn later that his motive has been to make her jealous:

Well I feigned courtship of Miss Ingram, because I wished to render you
as madly in love with me as I was with you; and I knew jealousy would
be the best ally I could call in for the furtherance of that end. (p.262)

As a plot device the visit helps to maintain suspense and provides a further obstacle to fulfilment. So far as the character of Jane is concerned, the episode casts her back into her old position of observer, on the fringes of life, noticing everything while unnoticed herself. There is poignancy in the stoicism of an unrequited lover, accepting pain without blaming the object of her love. She watches almost obsessively for some hint of attention or some acknowledgement from Rochester: " … how distant, how far estranged we were! So far estranged, that I did not expect him to come and speak to me" (p.174). The episode also repeats the contrast between vitality and stagnation, between the lifelessness of Blanche and her family and the vitality of Rochester:

I compared him with his guests. What was the gallant grace of the Lynns,
the languid elegance of Lord Ingram – even the military distinction of
Colonel Dent, contrasted with his look of native pith and genuine power?
… the light of the candles had as much soul in it as their smile; the tinkle
of the bell as much significance as their laugh. (p.175)

While Rochester appears to Jane almost as a force of nature, craggily powerful and bursting with suppressed energy, the others are feeble and superficial for all their good looks. This contrast is reminiscent of the same opposition in *Wuthering Heights*, where Heathcliff, as his name suggests, is the embodiment of a natural force while the Lintons are like feeble offshoots, over-refined by civilised manners.

Further periods of watching in the drawing room allow Jane to produce this devastating verdict on Blanche:

> Miss Ingram was a mark beneath jealousy: she was too inferior to excite the feeling. Pardon the seeming paradox: I mean what I say. She was showy, but she was not genuine: she had a fine person, many brilliant attainments; but her mind was poor, her heart barren by nature: nothing bloomed spontaneously on that soil … She was not good; she was not original: she used to repeat sounding phrases from books; she never offered, nor had, an opinion of her own. (pp. 185-6)

This is the beautiful but shallow woman that Jane believes will marry the man she has grown to love. Rochester has focused his gaze on Blanche; but his apparent lack of attention to Jane does not last. He requests her presence in the drawing room. He almost calls her *my love*, but bites his lip to stop himself. And soon afterwards, in another midnight crisis, it is Jane that he calls on for secret assistance.

Class difference

The difference in status is a difficult obstacle, and would certainly have been recognised as one by Victorian readers who were both conscious of its importance and excited by the notion of tearing the barriers down, at least in fiction. Nineteenth-century novels are full of heroes and heroines who defy convention and marry above their station, although it usually turns out that they are the secret children of noblemen or the heirs to great fortunes. *Jane Eyre* is no different, as we discover towards the end.

One notable exception is Becky Sharp in *Vanity Fair*. Thackeray's novel satirises a society which judges by appearances and whose values are based on wealth and status. Becky's ability to manipulate the vanity and stupidity of her superiors enables her to break through every social barrier; but while the reader admires her cleverness and laughs at her schemes, the author appears to intend her to be a warning, not an example to follow.

The secret wife

Class difference pales into insignificance beside the existence of the wife locked away in the attic. Brontë cleverly lays a trail of clues and possible explanations that create a genuine atmosphere of suspense and mystery.

What is behind the locked door? What is the reason for that disturbing laughter? Who is Grace Poole and why does she seem to come and go from the upper corridor? Who or what was the author of the fire, and the source of Mason's bloody wounds? This is the stuff of Gothic horror. It sharpens our curiosity and keeps us guessing; but its real significance for the relationship of Rochester and Jane appears only after Jane has been worn down by his persistence and agreed to marry him.

The happy couple are standing at the altar, with Jane on the threshold of fulfilment, about to marry the man she loves. The unexpected entrance of a lawyer breaking dreadful news spells the end of Jane's hopes and at a stroke resolves for the reader the mystery surrounding Rochester and his Gothic house.

Jane is left with a terrible dilemma. She has been accepted by Rochester but her acquiescence was secured by a lie. Rochester, Byronic as always, asks her to come abroad to live with him, but Jane will not accept the role of mistress, and, despite her real love for Rochester, she leaves Thornfield.

The outcast

Brontë presents Jane, after leaving Thornfield, as a lonely and destitute wanderer. It is the low point of her life's journey, forced to make a damp bed in the hillside bracken, famished yet ashamed to ask for a crust of bread, driven at last to offer her gloves for a cake but unable in the event to carry out her plan in the face of coldness and suspicion. Her reward for rejecting Rochester's suggestion is to be plunged into the purging wilderness of nature and to endure the scarifying contempt of her fellow men. Like so many heroes and heroines before her and after, from Lear to Tess Durbeyfield, her endurance is tested almost to breaking, but she emerges with her integrity unscathed. The natural environment, now sunny, now bleak, but always indifferent, emphasises her emotional landscape of loss and desolation. Although she is not afraid of nature and at first sees the heath as sympathetic to her plight ("Nature seemed to me benign and good: I thought she loved me" – p.323), she realises soon enough that she is an alien presence. To survive she must throw herself on the meagre charity of her fellow men: "I was a human being, and had a human being's wants: I must not linger where there was nothing to supply them" (p.324).

Humiliated and desperate, Jane begs for food but finds no sympathetic response and returns in the rain and twilight to the hills, now wilder and less appealing. The gleam of a distant light gives her hope, and she struggles wearily towards it like a pilgrim through the waste lands so beloved of Victorian writers, uttering an occasional prayer; soaked and chilled by the rain, splashing through the marsh, until exhausted she reaches the gate and falls at the door. As she gazes through the window into the comfortable kitchen with its peat fire and graceful occupants, we are reminded of Jane's position throughout the book, as an outsider looking in on the comfortable lives of others.

This waste-land interval, however, does not last. The spell is broken at the parsonage door, and with it the plight of Jane as a figure on the fringes of life. When the Rivers family act out their Christian principles and take the stranger into their house, it is as if the time of suffering and endurance has been rewarded by a listening deity.

In the period that follows Jane becomes more and more at one with the family, winning over the crusty housekeeper with her direct language and practical style, and relating to Diana and Mary like a sister.

When they first observe her they conclude that there is nothing "indicative of vulgarity or degradation" (p.339) in her countenance; but they also remark on her plainness. St John, always as blunt as Jane herself, concludes: "Ill or well, she would always be plain" (ibid.).

The Rivers family, however, unlike the Reed household, do not judge the stranger by her lack of outward beauty. They receive her into their family without hesitation. For the first time in her life's journey Jane experiences the acceptance and fulfilment of family life:

> The more I knew of the inmates of Moor House, the better I liked them. In a few days I had so far recovered my health that I could sit up all day, and walk out sometimes. I could join Diana and Mary in all their occupations; converse with them as much as they wished, and aid them when and where they would allow me. There was a reviving pleasure in this intercourse, of a kind now tasted by me for the first time – the pleasure arising from perfect congeniality of tastes, sentiments, and principles. (p.349)

This is significant not only in the development of Jane's character but also in plot terms because, as it conveniently turns out, Jane and the Rivers family are related; they are cousins, and it is through them that she learns of her inheritance. Before the reader is given this information, Brontë appears to offer her heroine, in the person of St John, an alternative future to the one set out by Rochester. St John is the complete opposite of Rochester, even in appearance. While Rochester is plain and stocky with irregular features, St John is tall and handsome with piercing blue eyes. More importantly they contrast in character. Where Rochester is full of suppressed energy, given to outbursts of feeling and instant decisions, St John is fiercely controlled. On the other hand they are also very similar, in that both are deeply passionate in nature. St John's passion, however, is channelled uncompromisingly into his missionary enterprise. This would be admirable (and indeed Jane does admire his dedication) if he did not also ruthlessly distort his own nature by setting aside his love for Rosamund.

> I love Rosamund Oliver so wildly – with all the intensity, indeed, of a first passion the object of which is exquisitely beautiful, graceful, and fascinating – I experience at the same time a calm, unwarped consciousness, that she would not make me a good wife. (p.373)

Jane gradually realises that it is the single-minded exercise of will over emotion that lies at the core of St John's character: "Reason, and not Feeling is my guide: my ambition is unlimited" (p.375). Unlike Brocklehurst, St John is not merely a nominal Christian: he acts out his Christian beliefs; but in his Christian ambition and zeal he makes the same mistake as Brocklehurst, driving a wedge between spiritual ambition and human nature:

> So much has religion done for me; turning the original materials to the best account: pruning and training nature. But she could not eradicate Nature nor will it be eradicated "till this mortal shall put on immortality". (p.376)

At first Jane is attracted to the heroic style of St John, and of course she has always been susceptible to the dominant male.

From St John she finds acceptance and the offer of a missionary role that appeals to her principles. But this appeal is not enough. In spite of constant pressure amounting to emotional blackmail, she cannot bring herself to fit in with his plans: "As for me, I daily wished more to please him: but to do so, I felt daily more and more that I must disown half my nature, stifle half my faculties" (p.398). His total acceptance is not unconditional; it depends on her adopting the role that he wishes for her, as his missionary wife. St John doesn't love Jane and doesn't care that she sees him only as a brother; he believes that she is the right person for the job and everything else must be sacrificed to that end.

The mysterious voice

At this point in the novel Brontë makes use again of a Gothic device. At just the moment when she is wrestling with St John's offer, Jane hears a mysterious voice calling to her. It is of course the voice of Rochester; and when she hears it the future becomes clear. The mysterious voice may also remind us of the 'Beauty and the Beast' fairy tale which underlies the story of Rochester and Jane. In the fairy tale, when Beauty goes home to her father, the beast extracts a promise that she will return after a few days. Her sisters prevent her from leaving, but in a dream she hears the dying beast calling her name. Like Beauty in the tale, Jane is determined to return.

When Jane finally leaves to seek out Rochester she does so as a changed woman. She has found a family, found acceptance as a family member and as a teacher. She has also learned that she is an heiress. If she returns to Rochester she will do so no longer as a servant, an inexperienced outsider, but as a confident woman.

Return to Thornfield

Jane leaves the man with the religious name and returns instead to Rochester, the namesake of a notorious Restoration rake.[5] The hero who is "mad, bad and dangerous to know" is more appealing to the romantic woman than the religious fanatic.

If Jane has been changed by her recent experience, so too has Rochester, and much more dramatically. He has been blinded in the Thornfield fire and his independence and dominance are gone: "The water stood in my eyes to hear this avowal of his dependence: just as if a royal eagle, chained to a perch, should be forced to entreat a sparrow to become its purveyor" (p.439).

One might say that Brontë has reduced him to a position that allows Jane to meet him as an equal, or indeed superior. She is healthy and has all the new-found confidence of financial independence: "And you are not a pining outcast among strangers?" says the blind Rochester. "No, sir; I am an independent woman now" (p.434). The sentence "Reader, I married him" has become one of the most famous in literature, partly because it illustrates a technique of confessional intimacy between narrator and reader, but also because it rings with a triumphant assertion of fulfilment against all the odds. The despised orphan, the plain outsider, the repressed schoolgirl, the watching servant has become the princess, giving her hand, not out of desperation, but because she recognises that Rochester, his restless spirit tamed, has come to depend entirely upon her.

NOTES

1 'Gothic novel' refers to a popular genre of stories which began to appear in the eighteenth century and remained popular well into the Victorian period. Typically they were set in castles and monasteries. They dealt in horror, ghostly apparitions and mystery. See p.123 of the novel.

2 See for instance Margot Peters, *Unquiet Soul: A Biography of Charlotte Brontë* (Hodder & Stoughton, 1975).

3 See Bruno Bettelheim, *The Uses of Enchantment: The Meaning and Importance of Fairy Tales* (Penguin, 1978).

4 Byron's poem *Childe Harold's Pilgrimage* was published between 1812 and 1818. Its hero, an attractive, enigmatic traveller, was identified with the author and became the source of great fascination to readers, propelling Byron to celebrity. In his own words, "I woke and found myself famous."

5 John Wilmot, second Earl of Rochester, was born in 1647 and died at the age of 33. He was a poet of real talent, especially in his *Satires*, and a courtier in the service of Charles II, and known as a fashionable wit and libertine.

3

Nature and Control

Nature plays an important part in *Jane Eyre*, both as vividly described wild elements and landscapes, and as the deepest selves of the characters. There is a continual tension in the story between nature (in these senses) and restriction or control. This tension is also related to the importance of religious belief and morality on the one hand and unrestricted licence on the other. Jane treads a difficult path as she matures, staying true to her beliefs and moral code, while trying to preserve her essential nature without distortion.

Jane's progress is in part an education in curbing her passionate nature and conforming to the will of God. Helen Burns, her friend at Lowood, is one of her moral instructors. When Jane complains in violent language about lack of love, Helen scolds her:

Hush, Jane! You think too much of the love of human beings; you are too impulsive, too vehement: the sovereign Hand that created your frame, and put life into it, has provided you with other resources than your feeble self, or than creatures feeble as you. (p.69)

Jane learns from Helen and from Miss Temple; and as the novel moves on, the key decisions and crises in her progress are always accompanied by a prayer or a reference to spiritual guidance:

I tired of the routine of eight years in one afternoon. I desired liberty; for liberty I gasped; for liberty I uttered a prayer, it seemed scattered on the wind then faintly blowing. I abandoned it, and framed a humbler supplication; for change, stimulus: that petition, too seemed swept off into vague space; "Then," I cried, half desperate, "grant me at least a new servitude!" (p.85)

Jane curbs her natural impulse for total freedom and prays for servitude; and servitude is what she gets, first as a servant, later as a loving wife, serving the crippled Rochester.

When she returns to Gateshead to visit the dying Mrs Reed she offers her former persecutor her full forgiveness, in keeping again with the ideals of a Christian life:

> "Love me, then, or hate me, as you will," I said at last, "you have my full and free forgiveness: ask now for God's; and be at peace." (p.240)

When Rochester's marriage is revealed and he persists in asking Jane to go away with him, she demonstrates the central importance of her moral principles by resisting both his request and his hopeless vision of a lonely future: "Do as I do: trust in God and yourself. Believe in heaven. Hope to meet again there" (p.316). The presentation is not trite. Jane is shown wrestling with her conscience and painfully deciding that she cannot agree to his pleas.

When she finally runs from the house to escape temptation, she prays with no sense of triumph or satisfaction. She has taken what she believes to be the right path; but it is a decision racked with grief and doubt:

> Gentle reader, may you never feel what I then felt! May your eyes never shed such stormy, scalding, heart-wrung tears as poured from mine. May you never appeal to Heaven in prayers so hopeless and so agonized. (p.322)

Jane resists the natural impulse to stay with the man she loves. The balance is difficult, but nature must be controlled. The alternative would be a life as Rochester's mistress, outside the moral law, and this she cannot accept.

The reader is introduced dramatically to passion out of control in the opening chapter of the novel, when the quarrelling children explode into violence. Brontë does not spare us the graphic detail. The style is vivid and direct: " ... the volume was flung, it hit me, and I fell, striking my head against the door and cutting it. The cut bled. The pain was sharp (p.11). The raw outbursts of passion from the Reed children are matched by Jane's as she attacks John and is carried kicking and protesting to the red-room.

These are childish passions, violent as they may be; but in the case of adults, being 'out of control' is associated with sexual dissipation, highlighted, in the Parisian liaisons of Rochester and the depravity of Bertha. Bertha also demonstrates the ultimate absence of control in her raving madness and the violence that goes with it: "The flesh on the shoulder is torn as well as cut? This wound was not done with a knife; there have been teeth here?" (p.212). When Rochester first expresses regret for his past and talks of the bitter taste of remorse, Jane encourages him towards Christian repentance: "Repentance is said to be its cure, sir" (p.136). But although Rochester is attracted by the idea of reforming his life, his way is blocked by an obstacle he cannot overcome. As he says, " ... since happiness is irrevocably denied me, I have a right to get pleasure out of life: and I *will* get it, cost what it may" (p.136). Jane acts as the voice of conscience. She is like the good angel in *Dr Faustus*,[1] reminding him honestly of the consequences of self-indulgence: "Then you will degenerate still more, sir" ; and again, "It will sting – it will taste bitter, sir"; and later, "Distrust it, sir, it is not a true angel" (p.136).

Rochester has chosen a difficult and immoral path because he has not restrained his natural inclinations. Eventually he recognises and confesses his faults; in time-honoured literary and Christian fashion, he must endure a period of hardship and suffer (literal) blindness to purge his nature, begin to see clearly and achieve the balance that Jane can reward with her hand: "I began to see and acknowledge the hand of God in my doom. I began to experience remorse, repentance, the wish for reconcilement to my Maker" (p.446). This is Rochester, confessing his new insight to Jane. On her return to Thornfield, Jane has discovered not only the man she fell in love with, but one who has been cleansed in the fire and has begun to think and feel as she does. She too has suffered yet the path taken has, by a winding route, led them both to true fulfilment.

Extreme control

On the other hand, too much control can distort and cripple nature. Jane does not condone licence, and sets about schooling Rochester in the moral life even as she is falling in love with him, but she clearly rejects the Helen Burns willingness to accept all restrictions on the natural impulse to seek happiness. The school at Lowood set out to crush the spontaneity, beauty and innocence in children in order to save them from sin. There is a similar distortion in the character of St John. His nature is passionate, but he ruthlessly represses it in the pursuit of his missionary zeal. Jane is profoundly disturbed by this distortion, and her realisation of its extent determines her return to Rochester.

The valuable nature

For Jane and her creator the essence of valuable nature is energy and spontaneity. Jane has it, Rochester has it and so do St John and his sisters; but characters such as Blanche, Mason and Elisa do not. They are described as lifeless and barren. The portrayal of Blanche is harsh. She is showy but false; she is accomplished but has a poor mind; her heart is barren. She never has an opinion of her own. The description is part of a central preoccupation in the novel that outward beauty is not a sign of value, just as plainness does not indicate a plain character or an ugly nature. Artificial manners have strangled the true vitality of these characters, until only a surface glitter survives.

One of the triggers for Jane's barrage of criticism is Blanche's dismissal of Adèle. This posing child is herself by no means a natural character in the mould of Jane or Rochester. If St John's nature is distorted by extreme control and Blanche's withered by fashionable manners, then Adèle's nature is marked by exaggerated gesture, self-consciousness and melodrama. She is described as a doll.

Imagery

Brontë uses several different types of image to suggest the distortion or the damming up of natural vitality. Before Jane feels able to shed her conventional governess manner she is described by Rochester as a caged bird: "I see at intervals the glance of a curious sort of bird through the close-set bars of the cage: a vivid, restless, resolute captive is there; were it free it would soar cloud high" (p.145). Elsewhere, Rochester's return to Thornfield brings life like a stream of fresh water in a barren place.

One of the most consistent images, recurring throughout the novel is the reference to stone, to suggest how the impulses of true nature have been petrified in certain characters, disabling them from acting with true feeling. Brocklehurst for instance is described as resembling a black pillar:

> I looked up at – a black pillar! – such, at least, appeared to me, at first sight, the straight narrow, sable-clad shape standing erect on the rug; the grim face at the top was like a carved mask, placed above the shaft by way of capital. (p.31)

This impression of hard darkness and inflexibility conveys his essential inhumanity.

Later in the story, St John is compared to white stone (p.392) and to a prostrate column. The reader is warned early in Jane's relationship with him that St John's nature is not likely to suit hers. Unlike his sisters, and unlike Jane herself, he is out of tune with the natural world of moor and heath and mountain.

> Nature was not to him that treasury of delight it was to his sisters ... never did he seem to roam the moors for the sake of their soothing silence – never seek out or dwell upon the thousand peaceful delights they could yield. (p.351)

To a writer like Brontë, reared in the Yorkshire moors and steeped in the Romantic poets, an absence of sympathy with nature amounted to a flaw in character. The man who cages and desiccates his true nature risks cutting himself off from sources of spiritual delight and from his fellow men.

This is the paradox that all who pursue an ideal must face. Even if the ideal, like St John's, is to help one's fellow men, its pursuit at the expense of one's own nature can be destructive: A line from a 20th-century poet expresses the problem: "Too long a sacrifice can make a stone of the heart" (from 'Easter 1916' by W.B. Yeats). In this poem Yeats struggles with the paradox that while he wants to celebrate the heroic sacrifice of the Irish republicans, he is aware that they have become inhuman in the pursuit of their ideals.

In the wider landscape of the novel it is also possible to sense the author's distrust of the huge rambling houses, the unnatural piles of brick and stone that her heroine is forced to inhabit. Jane wanders in them like a lost spirit searching for its true home.

In Gateshead there are no homely spaces; in Lowood only Miss Temple's small comfortable room provides an oasis of warm human feeling to soothe Jane's spirit. She is most at home in Moor House; the comfortable cottage home of the Rivers family: "They loved their sequestered home. I too, in the gray, small, antique structure ... found a charm, both potent and permanent" (p.349). By contrast Thornfield is cold, empty and frightening. Its vast rooms and corridors diminish its inhabitants, and even when Rochester returns, there is only one small area that takes on human dimensions, where Rochester sits by the fire and where Jane's pent-up nature can feel free and at home.

It is fitting that at the close of the novel Jane returns to a ruined Thornfield. The burned-out house is a symbol of its crippled owner. But its destruction is satisfying to the reader. Jane and Rochester take up their lives in a dwelling that has a more human scale, one that complements rather than imprisons their natures.

The imprisoned nature is a recurring theme and one setting in particular helps suggest it. Jane is often described peering out through the window in discontent, usually at a wild or seductive landscape that she finds more appealing than the confines of Gateshead or Lowood or even of Thornfield before the appearance of Rochester:

> I went to my window, opened it and looked out … My eye passed all other objects to rest on those most remote, the blue peaks. It was those I longed to surmount; all within their boundary of rock and heath seemed prison ground, exile limits. I traced the white road winding round the base of one mountain, and vanishing in a gorge between two. How I longed to follow it farther! (p.85)

Jane feels trapped and constricted. She longs for a fulfilling life, which is identified here in a recognisably human way with the winding road and the glowing distant landscape. By the close of the story Jane realises that she can express her nature freely only with Rochester, who has himself learned to accept the restrictions of his disability and embrace a more disciplined life.

NOTES

1   In Christopher Marlowe's play a good angel attempts to argue Dr Faustus away from temptation. See for example Act 1, Scene 1.

4

Women: Silent, Frustrated, Rebellious

The historical background to Brontë's portrayal of women is, in a nutshell, the absence of opportunity in a patriarchal society. The disadvantage was ingrained in the social fabric, but that did not hinder dissent by many women, including Charlotte Brontë. *Jane Eyre* reflects the social structure but it also expresses a spirit of rebellion.

There are no completely independent women in this novel, no free agents determining their own destiny, until the final chapters, when Jane learns that she is a wealthy woman. Interestingly she uses this knowledge not to launch out on an independent life but to return to marry the crippled Rochester, because now she can do so on equal terms. Brontë's preference, a radical one at the time, is for a marriage of equals, not a marriage of male dominance; but even for Brontë, marriage is the natural conclusion for a female life.

A husband's will

Mrs Reed provides us with a first and negative example of the married woman's predicament. Although she is portrayed as the wicked stepmother, she is a widow, whose husband has left her with burdens that she can scarcely bear: not only her own three children but also an unwanted orphan.

On the one hand, Mrs Reed is a useful narrative device from fairy tale, helping to form Jane's rebellious spirit; on the other, she is a realistic 19th-century widow, whose life is ruled by her husband's dead hand. Brontë allows the reader to experience this view of the widow when the adult Jane returns to Gateshead Hall to visit the dying Mrs Reed. She is generous to her old tormentor, who in the fever of her last illness reveals how difficult it was to accept her husband's bequest: "I have had more trouble with that child than anyone would believe. Such a burden to be left on my hands" (p.231).

Almost independent

In the early stages of the novel the closest we get to an independent woman is the character of Miss Temple, who runs the school. She is kind, educated, sensitive and sympathetic. She does her best to provide relief to Jane and Helen Burns from the cruelty of other teachers and from the miserable regime imposed by Brocklehurst. Although she has a professional presence and a management role, her power is limited and her status as an independent woman is short-lived. She too, like most contemporary women of the period, ultimately prefers marriage and domestic anonymity to the public life of the solitary wage-earner. After a few years in the school she marries a curate and disappears from the story. For all but a small percentage of women in the early 19th century the combination of married life and a career was not an option.

The marriage market

Characters such as Blanche Ingram, Georgiana Reed and Rosamund Oliver represent the class of women whom many an ordinary 19th-century girl would have aspired to emulate. They are bred to be elegant, taught to draw, to play the piano, to make polite conversation and ultimately to marry a rich husband. Many writers of the 19th century, including Thackeray and Tennyson, wrote about this aspect of marriage in the upper middle classes and aristocracy.[1] They criticised the custom of marriage made for money instead of love. Brontë, especially in her presentation of Blanche, is making the same case. Blanche is confident and educated; but she lacks substance. She tries to dominate Rochester's drawing room, but in fact she is only a counter in a larger game being played by her family in an effort to maintain their fortunes. Rochester lets Jane into the secret: "I caused a rumour to reach her that my fortune was not a third of what was supposed, and after that I presented myself to see the result: it was coldness both from her and her mother" (p.254). It is ironic that Blanche chooses to mock Adèle for her posing, childish affectation and anxiety to please, since she is in training to be just the kind of woman that Blanche represents: apparently independent, but in reality groomed for the marriage market and having no future without it.

The talented governess

Jane and the characters of Diana and Mary represent a different type of woman, one whose life Charlotte knew well, that of the governess. For an educated young woman in the 19th century, with no personal fortune and no immediate marriage prospects, the position of governess provided some security, a measure of independence from family and an opportunity to move in a sector of society more prosperous and privileged than her own.

Diana and Mary Rivers are staying with St John when Jane stumbles into their lives; but this spell at home is only a temporary one; each supports herself by working for a wealthy family in the south. Brontë takes great pains to show how genuinely accomplished these sisters are, with their wide and deep reading, their ability to debate and discuss, and their command of languages. Jane, who is an educated woman herself, likes nothing better than to sit and learn at their feet.

But the emphasis also suggests something else: the predicament of women who are full of life and energy, who have qualities of leadership in addition to knowledge as impressive as any man's, and yet whose talent goes unrecognised by all but their closest families:

> Diana and Mary were soon to leave Moor House, and return to the far different life and scene which awaited them, as governesses, in a large, fashionable, south-of-England city; where each held a situation in families, by whose wealthy and haughty members they were regarded only as humble dependants, and who neither knew nor sought one of their innate excellences. (p.352)

The governess moves in a world that most ordinary women would never experience: she mixes with the rich and privileged; she lives in a great house and is entrusted with the education of the children. This may seem a satisfying and fulfilling life. In some cases it was, but Brontë's presentation of Mary and Diana suggests the opposite. They appear privileged but in reality they are treated as servants, instruments rather than people. The fascinating inner lives of the sisters remain unknown to their employers, just as Jane's would have remained hidden if Rochester had not been a rebel, careless enough of social convention to think of marrying her.

When Blanche Ingram and her family come to Thornfield Brontë puts into their mouths a condescending, almost contemptuous view of the governess. While Jane looks on from the alcove, they reminisce about the pathetic creatures they have known. They laugh at the tricks they played on these servants and the discomfort they inflicted:

… I have just one word to say of the whole tribe: they are a nuisance. Not that I ever suffered much from them: I took care to turn the tables. What tricks Theodore and I used to play on our Miss Wilsons, and Mrs Greys and Madame Jouberts! (p.177)

Discontent and rebellion

Although *Jane Eyre* is not a feminist manifesto,[2] the book testifies to a strong desire to change the conventional role of women in their relations with men and society in general. The reader has no doubt that the author's dissatisfaction with the position of passive companion is strong.

When Jane talks bluntly to St John about his relationship with Rosamund, the young clergyman is surprised and shocked: "He had not imagined that a woman would dare to speak so to a man" (p.374). As Rochester learns, Jane is nothing if not direct and honest, and she herself says: "I felt at home in this sort of discourse." She is not prepared to adopt the conventional reserve expected in polite society, although she remains the passive observer when not in close dialogue with Rochester.

Brontë has presented Helen Burns as an important model for Jane; but ultimately it is not Helen's brand of silent acceptance that characterises the spirit of *Jane Eyre*: it is the voice of discontent and rebellion that first showed itself in the Reed household. The most passionate expression of discontent and the most revealing occurs after Jane's move to Thornfield and before the arrival of its master:

> It is in vain to say human beings ought to be satisfied with tranquillity: they must have action; and they will make it if they cannot find it. Millions are condemned to a stiller doom than mine, and millions are in silent revolt against their lot. Nobody knows how many rebellions besides political rebellions ferment in the masses of life which people live on earth. Women are supposed to be very calm generally; but women feel just as men feel; they need exercise for their faculties and a field for their efforts as much as their brothers do; they suffer from too rigid a restraint, too absolute a stagnation. (p.109)

Here are the rebellious Jane and the rebellious Charlotte at their most intense. The character speaks not only for herself but for all the millions of 19th-century women whose hopes and dreams were ignored and unfulfilled. The most heart-rending aspect of the appeal is the protest against the misguided idea that women do not have dreams and ambitions.

Fortunately for the heroine, Rochester's own unconventionality and rebelliousness allow her to express her true nature. She is not disregarded, not kept at a convenient distance, but encouraged and drawn out in a way that many a Victorian servant could only dream of.

The social outcasts

We meet many other types of women in the novel: teachers like the cruel Miss Scatcherd, servants like Bessie who can be cold and unhelpful but usually try to make Jane's childhood and future journey more bearable. There are also the social outcasts, the fallen women, mistresses and unfaithful wives, whom we hear about in Rochester's reminiscences and meet in the flesh in Bertha. These women would be the most difficult for any early 19th-century writer to include; it is not surprising that Rochester's French mistress remains a shadowy caricature, while Bertha is turned into a monster, a powerful narrative device whose psychology is not explored in any realistic way. Charlotte Brontë may be a rebel, but her scope for rebellion was restricted by the tolerance of publishers and readers.

NOTES

1   See Thackeray's *Vanity Fair*, published in the same year as Jane Eyre, 1847; also Tennyson's *Maud* (1855).

2   *A Vindication of the Rights of Women* by Mary Wollstonecraft is regarded as the text that gave women's rights an irrevocable place on the social and political agenda. It was published in 1792, 55 years before *Jane Eyre*.

5

The Madwoman and the Presentation of Feelings

Although we are continually aware of Jane's feelings, her sadness, her anger, her restlessness, it is clear that some areas of passionate feeling are more difficult to express in fiction than others. Jane's growing love for Rochester is the central example, and it is in this regard that the character of Bertha is crucial. In simple terms, Bertha is a monstrosity created to strengthen the Gothic element of the novel. She is the stand-in for the ghosts and mad monks of the classic Gothic tales. She is the raging fiend, the Frankenstein's monster in the farthest reaches of the castle, who adds a stab of mystery to the atmosphere and builds up suspense before the doomed wedding through her sudden destructive appearances. She laughs hideously in the dead of night outside Jane's room; she sets fire to Rochester's bedchamber; she appears beside Jane on the night before the wedding and tears the wedding veil.

Jane and the reader slowly become aware of her disturbing presence and we, like the heroine herself, are puzzled by the mystery. Is she a phantom or a terrible reality? Why is she there? What relationship does she have with Rochester? Why is she chained and locked away? What kind of violence is she capable of?

> What crime was this that lived incarnate in this sequestered mansion, and could neither be expelled nor subdued by the owner? – What mystery, that broke out now in fire and now in blood, at the deadliest hours of night? (p.210)

This is Jane, waiting with the wounded Mason for Rochester's return, hearing the animal sounds from the adjoining room and building up a sense of fear and horror with her questioning imagination.

The mystery gradually unfolds, dominating the Thornfield section of the novel, and ultimately revealing itself as not supernatural at all but instead a sordid piece of reality and a complete impediment to Jane's marriage.

However, while Bertha has this narrative function, she also heightens and even provides a symbol for Jane's imprisoned life, her hidden feelings, and especially the passionate disturbance that she experiences as her relationship with Rochester develops.[1] The madwoman is real but is also a symbol of something unsettling and hidden: the passionate feelings of women, especially their sexual desires. The difficulty of 19th-century novelists in expressing these reflects the conventional attitudes of the time, the pretence that such feelings do not exist, and if they do they must be concealed.

Charlotte Brontë was a child of Romanticism. The Romantic poets and novelists were interested in exploring the feelings of individuals and the mysterious dark regions of the mind that we call the subconscious. Coleridge's 'Ancient Mariner' is concerned with guilt and redemption but there is no rational debate. The weird seascapes of the poem throw onto the page disturbing nightmare landscapes that reflect the feelings of the guilty man wrestling with his conscience.

Again, in the opening chapters of *Wuthering Heights*, Emily Brontë establishes the visitor/narrator as a superficial figure from the city, with smooth and mild manners to match. But when he dreams of the ghost of Cathy tapping at his window, breaks the pane, grabs the fragile wrist and scrapes it on the splintered glass, the sudden violence suggests disturbing passions below the surface of the 'civilised' man.

Similarly Bertha's appearances are associated with disturbance of feeling in Jane. Initially when she wanders the corridors of Thornfield lonely and discontented, the strange peals of laughter seem to reflect her bleak restlessness. However, as the novel progresses, the appearances coincide with Jane's growing love for Rochester and the turmoil of emotion that this brings about. In Chapter 15 of the first volume Brontë describes the intimate conversations and the closeness that have developed between Rochester and Jane. Jane herself is falling in love, and her feelings are presented in positive phrases: "Keen delight ... so happy ... gratitude and many associations all pleasurable and genial made his face the object I liked best to see" (pp.145-6). These phrases are all suggestive of the happiness of new love; but they do not suggest the passionate disturbance that is also a feature of sexual attraction.

Immediately after this section Jane is woken in the dead of night by sinister laughter, and her investigation uncovers the fire in Rochester's room. It is as if Bertha has supplied the element of disturbance and danger that lies below the surface of growing love. The episode ends as Jane and her master stand together in their nightclothes and Rochester utters the wish that Jane would stay.

This symbolic presentation of Jane's feeling continues as she dreams of being tossed on a stormy sea, glimpsing now the shores of married bliss but then being blown back by powerful winds: "A counteracting breeze blew off land, and continually drove me back. Sense would resist delirium: judgement would warn passion" (p.151). The imagery of the natural elements contending in Jane, and driving her towards and then away from land is much more successful in conveying emotional conflict than any literal account of her thoughts.

This is one of several dream episodes in the novel that work to throw directly onto the page the contours of Jane's feeling. The combination of the madwoman's apparitions and dream imagery gives author and reader access to the hidden roots of inner turmoil.[2]

NOTES

1   See Sandra M. Gilbert and Susan Gubar, *The Madwoman in the Attic: The Woman Writer and the Nineteenth-Century Literary Imagination* (Yale University Press, 1979; reprinted 2000) for a detailed discussion of this and related issues.

2   See also references to Jane's drawings and paintings as devices to suggest her emotional landscape.

6

Realism and Romance

From the time of its publication, *Jane Eyre* was praised for realism in the psychology of its heroine and the detailed presentation of ordinary life; but the novel is also intensely romantic, with an unusual love story at its heart and a narrative embroidered with the trappings of Gothic fantasy. What are we to make of this blend?

It is not easy – or indeed useful – to formulate hard and fast definitions of realist and Romantic novels, but there are some distinctions that may help. Realist novels are largely concerned with narratives of everyday experiences, showing how characters' lives are shaped and dominated by work, family, money and social conventions. The pioneers of 19th-century realism in England, authors like Mrs Gaskell, set out to show the hardships of working-class life to the reading public. The opening chapters of *Mary Barton* provide vivid examples of this kind of realism.[1] George Eliot, perhaps the greatest of the 19th-century realists, is less preoccupied with poverty and squalor, but her finest work, *Middlemarch* for instance, is focused on the ways in which economic and social circumstances influence, for better or worse, the plans and dreams of her characters. She is one of the first novelists to present married life as a less than perfect experience, and to show in detail how a man can begin his career with high ideals only to be forced by his situation to compromise.[2]

Romantic novels are much more interested in the extraordinary. The fate of their characters is not governed so much by the common pressures of life as by strange and fantastical occurrences, by coincidence and sometimes supernatural intervention. Their people are often larger than life; they are strange or driven by forces that transcend the everyday influences of work and family relationships. *Wuthering Heights* is a Romantic novel in this sense, as is Mary Shelley's *Frankenstein.*[3]

We must not make the mistake of seeing realist and Romantic as opposites. Many 19th-century novels contain elements of each genre;

and consequently they respond to the desire of readers to experience both a reflection of their ordinary lives and a presentation of attractive ideals, strong emotion, spiritual reality and the supernatural.

In some cases the impact of a novel's realism can be undermined by its Romantic qualities. Mrs Gaskell's *Mary Barton* is, I believe an example of this. It is an interesting question whether the same is true of Charlotte Brontë's *Jane Eyre*.

A visitor from the grave

In the Gateshead section of the novel our attention is focused on the entirely realistic experience of an unwanted child whose fate has been decided by her dead father's wishes. Although we feel the influence of the Cinderella story, this only serves to render more powerful the psychological realism of the stepmother–stepdaughter tension and the violence of sibling rivalry. There is no fairy godmother at this stage of the tale, although the echo of 'Cinderella' does establish hope in the reader that one may emerge in the future.

The only suggestion of a Romantic device occurs in the red-room episode, when Jane sees a gleam of light on the ceiling and imagines that it may be a visitor from beyond the grave coming to comfort her. Brontë cleverly undermines this possibility by having the narrator (Jane) suggest the realistic explanation, that it may only have been a lantern reflecting light from the garden. In this way, the author has it both ways, hinting at supernatural comfort while also providing a natural explanation.

The problem of Helen Burns

The Lowood experience is dominated by the kind of realistic detail that we find in Gaskell, descriptions of the harsh school regime, the wretched food, the lack of good clothing and comfort, the physical abuse and psychological sadism. Although Brontë did not intend it to be a social document, *Jane Eyre* certainly provides us with a striking piece of evidence about the charity schools of the period.

The only element that disturbs this account is the presentation of Helen Burns. Although Helen is a prime victim of the system, she is also idealised by Brontë in a way that modern readers cannot easily accept. Helen is a character who endures punishment without complaint and accepts her suffering as part of her Christianity. In itself this portrayal is not a problem: there are real people who have acted in this way. But there is a problem in the regular speeches that she delivers to Jane, which become uncomfortably like sermons. By making her so holy Brontë turns her into an embodiment of the infant Christ speaking with a wisdom inconceivable in a child of her age. No doubt Brontë failed to see Helen as an over-romanticised character because she was based on her own sister Mary. Helen is intended to be a key influence on Jane, but she is much more of an idealised voice than a realistic character, and her death, which should be a part of the Lowood realism, showing the consequences of neglect and cruelty, is portrayed with melodramatic sentimentality. If she does influence Jane, as Brontë must have intended, it is not clear where this influence is meant to appear. Jane remains restless, plain-speaking and a rebel almost to the end. D.H. Lawrence's words on the intentions of writers are apt here: "Never trust the teller; trust the tale."

The Byronic hero and the madwoman

The Thornfield sections of the novel are the most Romantic in every sense. At the centre is the love growing between Jane and Rochester accompanied by the stock appurtenances of the Gothic novel: the rambling castle-like house, the secret rooms, the strange sounds and apparitions, the monstrous presence in the attic. Rochester himself is a hero out of Byron, a man with a mysterious past, an outsider, a wanderer on the face of the earth, dark and brooding, a man with a terrible burden whose weight can be eased only by the love of a pure woman. However, Rochester is saved from becoming a Romantic caricature by his interaction with Jane's plain common sense and by the detailed descriptions of his past, which provide motivation, in a way lacking in the presentation of Heathcliff in *Wuthering Heights*.

The apparently supernatural events grip the reader's imagination and build up suspense. They turn out of course to have a rational explanation; but the character of the madwoman remains a fantastical and extreme one. Bertha, as a West Indian, is not only exotic and guaranteed to disturb the Victorian reader by that very fact, but she is also given a full set of extreme and shocking qualities.

When Rochester describes his first sight of Bertha she appears beyond reproach: "I found her a fine woman, in the style of Blanche Ingram; tall, dark and majestic" (p.321). But having married her, apparently in a blind infatuation, he soon realised that his wife's character was "wholly alien to mine; her tastes obnoxious to me; her cast of mind common, low, narrow and singularly incapable of being led to anything higher" (p.305). But that is not the worst. He soon discovers that Bertha is totally debauched:

her vices sprung up fast and rank … What a pigmy intellect she had and what giant propensities! How fearful were the curses those propensities entailed on me! Bertha Mason, the true daughter of an infamous mother, dragged me through all the hideous and degrading agonies which must attend a man bound to a wife at once intemperate and unchaste … a nature the most gross, impure, depraved I ever saw, was associated with mine. (p.306)

His wife has turned out to be a monster. It is made abundantly clear that she is sexually insatiable. Rochester tells Jane the medical verdict: "The doctors now discovered that my wife was mad – her excesses had prematurely developed the germs of insanity" (p.306).

Although there is plenty of detail, which helps to exonerate Rochester in Jane's eyes, the account of Bertha's character lacks subtlety. To portray Bertha as a nymphomaniac is extreme enough; to make her insane as well puts her into the monster category fitting for a Gothic horror story. She is presented only as a grotesque fiend, and no attempt is made to provide a realistic human dimension.

Coincidence

Coincidence is a narrative device familiar in Romantic novels, and in the penultimate section of *Jane Eyre* there are two coincidences, vital to the plot and to the novel's positive ending, which strain the bounds of realism. The first is the circumstance that of all the cottages in all the counties of North and Middle England, Jane happens to collapse at the door of the one owned by her unknown cousins; and the second is the fact that, at this opportune moment, an uncle of whom she has barely heard dies abroad and leaves her a fortune. Overnight she is changed from an impoverished governess to the independence of a rich woman. It is a transformation worthy of fairy tales which turn the ragged servant into a princess. It is a wish-fulfilment dream for every reader. As a consequence, Jane is able to return to Rochester as his equal.

In the final section, after Jane returns to Thornfield there is no romance in the predicament of Rochester. The grim but energetic master of old is now a pathetic figure, crippled, blind and melancholy, at least until Jane's devotion and care restore him to full life. However this Romantic fulfilment is accomplished by a final incident that strains credulity: the reader learns about the dramatic fire that conveniently kills Bertha and leaves Rochester both free to marry and enfeebled enough to need Jane's care.

First-person narrative

The literary device that allows the successful blend of realism with the occasional oddity of romance is the first-person narrative. Jane herself tells the story. It is reassuring to the reader to know that the character who has come through hardship and danger has emerged to tell the tale. But the narrative voice also manages to persuade us that the weirdest events can fall within the realm of experience. We are convinced by its delicate observation and sensitive judgements. It is a voice both thoughtful and sensible. It is capable of anger and of remorse; it is sympathetic but often direct. It explores motive, it attempts to understand. It is often self-critical.

The reader is drawn to trust its honesty and evidently sincere feeling, and prepared to accept almost anything that it relates. Take for instance the episode at Thornfield in which Rochester pretends to be an old gypsy. Jane moves us into this unlikely scene in exactly the same matter-of-fact way that she uses to take us into the drawing room with Blanche Ingram; she talks to the old crone in the same direct and lively style she uses with Rochester. The notion that Jane would be fooled by the disguise is ludicrous; but the narrative method helps us to suspend disbelief.

NOTES

1   *Mary Barton* was published in 1848, a year after *Jane Eyre.*

2   Dr Lydgate comes to the town of Middlemarch, determined to follow the highest medical ideals. He marries Rosamund Vincy, a beautiful girl who does not share his notion of what is important in life, and his future follows a very different path from the one he had planned, a path of compromise and disillusionment. *Middlemarch* was published in 1871-2.

3   *Frankenstein* was published in 1818.

7

Last Words

Charlotte Brontë's novel has remained popular for over 150 years. It is studied in universities and schools and read for pure enjoyment, as well as being used for numerous films and television serials. Clearly it has found the formula for a successful novel. Perhaps this has to do with the timeless appeal of the Cinderella figure Jane, the plain girl, whose destiny is to defy her difficult start in life and through a hard journey to find love and fulfilment. The story is written in a direct and vigorous style, and the theme is guaranteed to appeal, touching as it does on essential human hopes and dreams. This is a part of the answer but only a part.

In this study I have tried to suggest some of the other reasons for the continuing appeal of *Jane Eyre*. The exploration is not exhaustive; its aim is to encourage readers to return to the novel itself with renewed interest, and with ideas of their own on the topics I have discussed and on those that have only been hinted at.

Further Reading

Juliet Barker, *The Brontës*, Weidenfeld & Nicolson, London, 1994.

Bruno Bettleheim, *The Uses of Enchantment: The Meaning and Importance of Fairy Tales*, Penguin, London, 1978.

Harold Bloom, ed., *Charlotte Brontë's Jane Eyre: Modern Critical Interpretations*, Chelsea House, New York, 1987.

Elizabeth Gaskell, *The Life of Charlotte Brontë*, 1857, reprinted Oxford University Press, Oxford, 1974.

Sandra Gilbert and Susan Gubar, *The Madwoman in the Attic: The Woman Writer and the Nineteenth-Century Literary Imagination*, Yale University Press, New Haven and London, 1979; reprinted 2000.

Q.D. Leavis, Introduction to *Jane Eyre*, Penguin, London, 1966.

Sara Lodge, *Charlotte Brontë – Jane Eyre: A Reader's Guide to Essential Criticism*, Palgrave Macmillan, London, 2009.

Margot Peters, *Unquiet Soul: A Biography of Charlotte Brontë*, Hodder & Stoughton, London, 1975.

Margaret Smith, ed., *Jane Eyre*, Introduction and revised notes by Sally Shuttleworth, Oxford World's Classics, Oxford, 2000.

GREENWICH EXCHANGE BOOKS

STUDENT GUIDE LITERARY SERIES

The Greenwich Exchange Student Guide Literary Series is a collection of essays on major or contemporary serious writers in English and selected European languages. The series is for the student, the teacher and the 'common reader' and is an ideal resource for libraries. The *Times Educational Supplement* praised these books, saying, "The style of [this series] has a pressure of meaning behind it. Readers should learn from that ... If art is about selection, perception and taste, then this is it."

The series includes:

Antonin Artaud by Lee Jamieson (978-1-871551-98-3)
W.H. Auden by Stephen Wade (978-1-871551-36-5)
Jane Austen by Pat Levy (978-1-871551-89-1)
Honoré de Balzac by Wendy Mercer (978-1-871551-48-8)
Louis de Bernières by Rob Spence (978-1-906075-13-2)
William Blake by Peter Davies (978-1-871551-27-3)
The Brontës by Peter Davies (978-1-871551-24-2)
Robert Browning by John Lucas (978-1-871551-59-4)
Lord Byron by Andrew Keanie (978-1-871551-83-9)
Samuel Taylor Coleridge by Andrew Keanie (978-1-871551-64-8)
Joseph Conrad by Martin Seymour-Smith (978-1-871551-18-1)
William Cowper by Michael Thorn (978-1-871551-25-9)
Charles Dickens by Robert Giddings (987-1-871551-26-6)
Emily Dickinson by Marnie Pomeroy (978-1-871551-68-6)
John Donne by Sean Haldane (978-1-871551-23-5)
Elizabethan Love Poets by John Greening (978-1-906075-52-1)
Ford Madox Ford by Anthony Fowles (978-1-871551-63-1)
Sigmund Freud by Stephen Wilson (978-1-906075-30-9)
The Stagecraft of Brian Friel by David Grant (978-1-871551-74-7)
Robert Frost by Warren Hope (978-1-871551-70-9)
Patrick Hamilton by John Harding (978-1-871551-99-0)
Thomas Hardy by Sean Haldane (978-1-871551-33-4)
Seamus Heaney by Warren Hope (978-1-871551-37-2)
Joseph Heller by Anthony Fowles (978-1-871551-84-6)

George Herbert By Neil Curry and Natasha Curry (978-1-906075-40-8)
Gerard Manley Hopkins by Sean Sheehan (978-1-871551-77-8)
James Joyce by Michael Murphy (978-1-871551-73-0)
Philip Larkin by Warren Hope (978-1-871551-35-8)
Laughter in the Dark – The Plays of Joe Orton by Arthur Burke
  (978-1-871551-56-3)
George Orwell by Warren Hope (978-1-871551-42-6)
Sylvia Plath by Marnie Pomeroy (978-1-871551-88-4)
Poets of the First World War by John Greening (978-1-871551-79-2)
Alexander Pope by Neil Curry (978-1-906075-23-1)
Philip Roth by Paul McDonald (978-1-871551-72-3)
Shakespeare's *A Midsummer Night's Dream* by Matt Simpson
  (978-1-871551-90-7)
Shakespeare's *As You Like It* by Matt Simpson (978-1-906075-46-0)
Shakespeare's *Hamlet* by Peter Davies (978-1-906075-12-5)
Shakespeare's *Julius Caesar* by Matt Simpson (978-1-906075-37-8)
Shakespeare's *King Lear* by Peter Davies (978-1-871551-95-2)
Shakespeare's *Macbeth* by Matt Simpson (978-1-871551-69-3)
Shakespeare's *The Merchant of Venice* by Alan Ablewhite (978-1-871551-96-9)
Shakespeare's *Much Ado About Nothing* by Matt Simpson
  (978-1-906075-01-9)
Shakespeare's Non-Dramatic Poetry by Martin Seymour-Smith
  (978-1-871551-22-8)
Shakespeare's *Othello* by Matt Simpson (978-1-871551-71-6)
Shakespeare's *Romeo and Juliet* by Matt Simpson (978-1-906075-17-0)
Shakespeare's Second Tetralogy: *Richard II–Henry V*
  by John Lucas (978-1-871551-97-6)
Shakespeare's Sonnets by Martin Seymour-Smith (978-1-871551-38-9)
Shakespeare's *The Tempest* by Matt Simpson (978-1-871551-75-4)
Shakespeare's *Twelfth Night* by Matt Simpson (978-1-871551-86-0)
Shakespeare's *The Winter's Tale* by John Lucas (978-1-871551-80-8)
Percy Bysshe Shelley by Andrew Keanie (978-1-871551-59-0)
Tobias Smollett by Robert Giddings (978-1-871551-21-1)
Alfred, Lord Tennyson by Michael Thorn (978-1-871551-20-4)
Dylan Thomas by Peter Davies (978-1-871551-78-5)
William Wordsworth by Andrew Keanie (978-1-871551-57-0)
W.B. Yeats by John Greening (978-1-871551-34-1)

FOCUS ON SERIES

FOCUS Series (ISBN prefix 978-1-906075 applies to all the following titles)

Other subjects covered by Greenwich Exchange books

Biography

Education

Philosophy